LECTIO DIVINA FOR YOUTH

JOHN

LECTIO DIVINA FOR YOUTH

ANCIENT FAITH SERIES

Barefoot Ministries®
Kansas City, Missouri

Copyright © 2008 by Barefoot Ministries®

ISBN 978-0-8341-5022-5

Written by Patricia J. David
Editor: Mike Wonch
Contributing Editor: Bo Cassell
Assistant Editors: Robyn M. Lowery and Jason Sivewright
Cover Design: JR Caines
Interior Design: Sharon Page

Adapted from *Lectio Divina Bible Studies: Listening for God Through John*.

David, Patricia J. *Lectio Divina Bible Studies: Listening for God Through John*. Indianapolis, IN: Wesleyan Publishing House and Beacon Hill Press of Kansas City, 2005.

Library of Congress Cataloging-in-Publication Data

David, Patricia J.
   Listening for God through John / written by Patricia J. David.
     p. cm. — (Ancient faith series)
   ISBN 978-0-8341-5022-5
  1. Bible. N.T. John—Devotional literature. 2. Bible. N.T. John—Textbooks. 3. Youth—Religious life. I. Title.

   BS2615.54.D38 2008
   226.5'00712—dc22

2007036249

ABOUT THE
LECTIO DIVINA
BIBLE STUDIES

Lectio divina (pronounced lek-tsee-oh dih-vee-nuh), is a Latin phrase that means *sacred reading.* It is the ancient Christian practice of communicating with God through the reading and study of Scripture. Throughout history, great Christian leaders have used and adapted this ancient method of interpreting Scripture.

The idea behind *lectio divina* is to look at a Bible passage in such a way that Bible study becomes less about study and more about listening. The approach is designed to focus our attention on what God is saying to us through the Word. Through the process of *lectio divina* we not only read to understand with our minds, but we read to hear with our hearts and obey. It is a way of listening to God through His Word.

Some throughout history have said that *lectio divina* turns Bible study on its head—normally we read the Bible, but in *lectio divina, the Bible reads us.* That is probably a good way to describe it. It is God using His Word in a conversation with us to read into our lives and speak to our hearts.

In this series, we will use the traditional *lectio divina* model. We have expanded each component so that it can be used by both individuals and by groups. Each session in this study includes the following elements. (Latin words and their pronunciation are noted in parentheses.)

- •**Reading** (*Lectio* "lek-tsee-oh"). We begin with a time of quieting ourselves prior to reading. Then we take a slow, careful look at a passage of Scripture. We focus our minds on the central theme of the passage. When helpful, we read out loud or read the same passage over and over several times.
- •**Meditation** (*Meditatio* "medi-tah-tsee-oh"). Next, we explore the meaning of the Bible passage. Here we dig deep to try to understand all of what God might be saying to us. We think on the

passage. We explore the images, and pay attention to the emotions and feelings that the passage provides. We put ourselves in the story. We look for particular words or phrases that leap off the page as the Spirit begins to speak to us through the Word.

•**Prayer** (*Oratio* "or-ah-tsee-oh"). As we meditate on the passage, we respond to God by communicating with Him. We specifically ask God to speak to us through His Word. We begin to dialog with Him about what we have read. We express praise, thanksgiving, confession, or agreement to God. And we listen. We wait before Him in silence, allowing God the chance to speak.

•**Contemplation** (*Contemplatio* "con-tehm-plah-tsee-oh"). At this point in our conversation through the Word, we come to a place where we rest in the presence of God. Our study is now about receiving what He has said to us. Imagine two old friends who have just talked at length—and now without words, they just sit together and enjoy each other's presence. Having spent time listening to God, we know a little better how God is shaping the direction of our lives. Here there is a yielding of oneself to God's will. We resolve to act on the message of Scripture.

GROUP STUDY

This book is designed to be useful for both individual and group study. To use this in a group, you may take one of several approaches:

•**Individual Study/Group Review**. Make sure each member of the group has a copy of the book. Have them read through one section during the week. (They will work through the same passage or portions of it each day that week.) Then, when you meet together, review what thoughts, notes, and insights the members of the group experienced in their individual study. Use the group questions at the end of the section as a guide.

•**Group Lectio**. Make sure each member of the group has a copy of the book. Have them read through one section during the week in individual study. When you meet together as a group, you will study the passage together through a reading form similar to lectio divina:

○First, read the passage out loud several times to the group. Group members respond by waiting in silence and letting God speak.

○Second, have the passage read aloud again to the group once or twice more. Use different group members for different voices, and have them read slowly. Group members listen for a word or two that speaks to them, and share it with the group. Break into smaller groups if appropriate.

○Third, read the passage out loud again, and have the group pray together to ask God what He might be saying to each person, and to the group as a whole. Go around and share what each person is learning from this process. At this point, review together the group questions at the end of the section.[1]

•Lectio Divina Steps for Groups. Make sure each member has a copy of the book. As a group, move through the study together, going through each of the parts: reading, mediation, prayer, and contemplation. Be sure to use the group questions at the end of the section.

The important thing about using *lectio divina* in a group is to remember that this is to be incarnational ("in the flesh")—in other words, we begin to live out the Word in our community. We carry God's Word in us, (in the flesh, or incarnate in us) and we carry that Word into our group to be lived out among them.

The *Lectio Divina Bible Studies* invite readers to slow down, read Scripture, meditate upon it, and prayerfully respond to God's Word.

---

1. Parts of the "Group Lectio" section adapted from Tony Jones, *The Sacred Way: Spiritual Practices for Everyday Life,* Grand Rapids: Zondervan, 2005, p. 54.

CONTENTS

INTRODUCTION

After the fall of Adam and Eve, God became distant and un-approachable—a God who seemed far off from the human race. But the coming of Jesus the Christ brought God close to people. He spoke to them, touched them, challenged their assumptions, and became involved in the messiest parts of their lives.

John, the author of the Gospel we'll be examining, was one of those closest to Jesus when He walked this earth. John was the son of Salome, who may have been the sister of Mary, Jesus' mother. John was also a member of Jesus' inner circle. So when John records and interprets the events of Jesus' life and ministry, we can be certain that he was reporting what he knew to be true.

Remember that John also wrote three letters (epistles) to the Early Church and, toward the end of his life, was witness and recorder of the events we read about in the Book of Revelation. According to John's account, the glorified Jesus gave him a glimpse at the events that would end human history.

The Gospel of John, written long after Matthew, Mark, and Luke, shows us the simplicity, significance, and mystery of

Jesus' words. Each story from the life of Jesus was chosen carefully to convince us of Jesus' deity and to show us the abundant life we can live in Him (John 20:31).

This book fits the good news into the popular verse: "For God so loved the world that he gave his one and only Son, that whoever believes in him shall not perish but have eternal life" (John 3:16). John's visual descriptions and powerful quotes from Jesus show how His bold commands can make a dramatic difference in both our lives today and our eternal destiny.

THE WORD INCARNATE
LISTENING FOR GOD THROUGH JOHN 1:1-18

SUMMARY

It had been 400 years since God had spoken to His people, the Israelites, through His prophets. Had He forgotten about them? Had His plan of redemption (salvation), created from the foundation of the world, ended?

He had promised a Messiah, a Redeemer, someone to free His people from oppression and to defeat Satan once and for all. Yet there was no sign of redemption in sight. The prophets had foretold it, but God was silent.

And then Jesus came, deity in human flesh. God himself entered His creation to show a lost people the way back to God, to free mankind from the penalty and power of sin.

God had spent a long time preparing His people for this event. The Law and the Prophets, the sacrifices and the feasts—all of Israel's history and tradition—had been pointing to His coming. Through this they would recognize it and grasp the fullness of its meaning.

But they missed it.

And many still do.

PREPARATION ✟ FOCUS YOUR THOUGHTS

When do you open your Christmas gifts?

Why is it so hard to wait until Christmas morning?

What kinds of secrets do you have difficulty keeping?

READING ✟ HEAR THE WORD

John's Gospel was written long after the others, possibly as late as A.D. 85. Matthew, Mark, and Luke give us the framework of Jesus' life and works, but John goes to a deeper level and shows us their meaning and purpose. Through his writing, John intends the reader to be drawn into a relationship with Christ. For example, John states, "Jesus did many other miraculous signs in the presence of his disciples, which are not recorded in this book. But these are written that you may believe that Jesus is the Christ, the Son of God, and that by believing you may have life in his name" (John 20:30-31).

Because the events surrounding Jesus' birth had already been recorded, John shows us the deeper meaning and reality behind those events in 1:1-18. He shows us that Jesus didn't come into existence on that first Christmas. He was no ordinary baby.

In John you will see words repeated for emphasis: *believe* (99 times), *life* (36 times), *witness/testify* (47 times), and *world* (78 times). The theme of light versus darkness is also repeated throughout. All of them are introduced in the first chapter.

Read John 1:1-18 slowly out loud. Be sure to pause between sentences, allowing yourself time to soak in the meaning. If you're involved in a group study, have a different person read the entire passage aloud without pausing. As you listen, ask God to impress a word or phrase on your mind—His Word for you today.

MEDITATION ✣ ENGAGE THE WORD

Meditate on John 1:1-5, 14, and 18

How does John 1:1 compare with Genesis 1:1? Why do you think John uses similar words? Why does John use "the Word" to describe Jesus? How else does he describe Jesus? In what ways was Jesus "light"? How is Jesus a "light" in your life?

John tells us Jesus *was* God and was *with* God at the same time. He also describes Jesus as "God the One and Only" in 1:18. How do you understand the concept of the Trinity (Father, Son, and Holy Spirit)? What, if anything, confuses you about the Trinity? Do you feel you have to understand this concept in order to believe it?

Read the quote by George Washington Carver. Do you think it's even possible for human beings to fully understand the nature of God? If we could grasp His nature, what would that say about God? What are your own personal questions you have about God's nature?

> When I was young, I said to God, "God, tell me the
> mystery of the universe." But God answered, "That
> knowledge is for me alone." So I said, "God, tell me the
> mystery of the peanut." Then God said, "Well, George,
> that's more nearly your size."
>
> —George Washington Carver

In what ways did Jesus make God known (1:18)? What characteristics of God did Jesus reveal that weren't evident in the Old Testament?

What did Jesus have to give up in order to be born into this world? How would you respond if someone asked you to give up something important to you in order to benefit others? In what ways was Jesus limited? How does it make you feel to know that God went to great lengths so that you would know who He is and how much He cares for you?

Meditate on John 1:10-13, 16-17

Which type of Messiah were the first-century Jews looking for? If Jesus fulfilled all the Old Testament prophecies concerning himself, why do you think so many people did not recognize Him? If you were living during that time, do you think you would have been able to recognize Him as the Messiah?

Do you agree with the quote from Pearl Bailey? What keeps people from recognizing God today? Do you find it hard to recognize God?

> People see God every day; they just don't recognize
> Him.   —Pearl Bailey

Do you think people "did not receive him" because they didn't realize who He was or because they *did* realize who He was, but *chose* not to put their trust in Him? In other words, was it because of ignorance, willfulness, or both?

What does Jesus offer to those who believe and receive Him? What does it mean to be a child of God? Do you live your life as if God is your father? Why do you think someone might deliberately choose *not* to become a child of God?

Meditate on John 1:6-9, 15

What do you know about John the Baptist? How is he described by the apostle John? How would you describe his attitude? What was the reaction to John's ministry (see John 10:41 and Matt. 14:1-12)? Do you think he ever considered *not* telling others about Jesus?

Jesus came as light into the world, and He calls us to be the "light of the world" (Matt. 5:14). What would the world be like without physical light? What would it be like if Jesus had never come? What would it be like if we didn't reflect the light of Christ in our world? How would your life be impacted if Christ wasn't lighting your paths?

Do you think John 3:20 accurately describe people today? Think about when you were still living in darkness. How did you feel about the light before you encountered Jesus? Who was the "John the Baptist" in your life who pointed you to Christ?

> Everyone who does evil hates the light, and will not come into the light for fear that his deeds will be exposed.   —John 3:20

PRAYER ✝ ASK AND LISTEN

Seek the face of God. Ask, "Lord, what are You saying to us today?"

Jesus came as light and life. He came to make God known. Spend some time in silent prayer and ask God to speak to your heart and make you aware of areas in your life that keep you from reflecting His light.

CONTEMPLATION ✝ REFLECT AND YIELD

Jesus had to give up all the splendor of heaven to come as a light to the world. What might God be asking you to sacrifice to be a light to your world? How willing are you to share the news of Christ with your friends and family?

GROUP STUDY

- What difference has Jesus coming to earth made? What if He had never been born?

- What does it mean that Jesus is "light"?

- How has Jesus been a light to your path, and given you direction when you needed it?

- Is it hard to be a light in our darkened world? What makes it so hard to share the good news?

- If your friends at school were asked if you had been reflecting the light of Jesus, how would they respond? Would you be satisfied with their answer?

- What are ways that you can make Jesus known?

- Make a list of four people who are part of your world. What can you say or do this week to show them Jesus?

YOU MUST BE BORN AGAIN

LISTENING FOR GOD THROUGH JOHN 3:1-18

SUMMARY

The Jewish people had always considered themselves special in the eyes of God—and rightly so. God had chosen them. He had redeemed them from slavery in Egypt with an incredible display of His power. He had given them the Ten Commandments and the Law. However, He never meant for them to be the only ones to receive His grace. His promise to Abraham had been, "All peoples on earth will be blessed through you" (Gen. 12:3).

Throughout history Israel welcomed converts. These people were said to have been "reborn" at the time they converted to the true faith of Judaism. The concept of being "born again" was not a new one. But when Jesus told a Jewish religious leader (Nicodemus) that he, too, had to be born again, it was revolutionary. The religious leader had a hard time grasping it.

God's infinite love for people isn't limited to the religious or moral. Jesus came to be a Savior for all who would believe—for all who would be born again.

PREPARATION ⚜ FOCUS YOUR THOUGHTS

What are some of the rules in your home?

How are your family's standards different from those of other families?

What are some of the rules in your church? In your youth group?

Over the years, how have the rules of the church and youth group changed?

READING ⚜ HEAR THE WORD

Word had gotten out about Jesus. He was in Jerusalem to celebrate the Passover (the celebration of God's deliverance of the Israelites from Egypt). Right after His encounter with Nicodemus, Jesus got rid of the money changers and merchants from the temple courts. He overturned their tables, and drove them out with a homemade whip—quite a display of zeal for God's house.

When the Jews questioned His actions, Jesus answered, "Destroy this temple, and I will raise it again in three days" (John 2:19). That got their attention. And so did His miracles. Many people saw and believed (John 2:23). It was time for an expert to check Him out.

The Jewish ruling council, called the Sanhedrin, was a group of 71 experts in the Law. They met in a chamber within the temple courts and governed the religious, political, and judicial life of the Jewish people. Of all the social groups serving on this council, the Pharisees were the most thorough in keeping the Law. They were considered to be righteous and devout. They even developed an elaborate system of 630 commands to make sure they never broke one of God's commandments. Nicodemus was a Pharisee, and he went to Jesus to find out for himself who this man was.

Read John 3:1-18. If you're studying in a group, choose one person to read the words of Jesus, and another to read the words of Nicodemus, and a third to read the narration. Have your narrator also read 3:16-18.

MEDITATION ✟ ENGAGE THE WORD

Meditate on John 3:1-8

Why do you think Nicodemus approached Jesus at night? Would you have approached Jesus in the same way that Nicodemus did? What do you think Nicodemus thought about Jesus before meeting Him? Why do you think Jesus responded to him so abruptly?

How did Jesus' understanding of the kingdom of God differ from the traditional understanding of the Jews? (See Luke 17:20-21.) What did Jesus say were the requirements for entering this kingdom? How would those requirements have been different from what the Pharisees thought them to be?

The term *born again* can also be translated *born from above*. Read the definition given by Oswald Chambers. How does that translation affect your understanding of the term?

> *Being born from above is a perennial, perpetual, and eternal beginning, a freshness all the time in thinking and in talking and in living, the continual surprise of the life of God.* —Oswald Chambers

How do you think Nicodemus felt when Jesus told him he wasn't good enough on his own to enter God's kingdom? How would you have responded if you were put in the place of Nicodemus?

What do you think Jesus meant when He said we must be

born of "water and the Spirit"? Does Ezekiel 36:24-27 help answer that question? In John 3:8 the word used for *Spirit* is the same word used for *wind*. How is the Spirit's work in the human heart similar to the wind?

Meditate on John 3:9-12

Nicodemus was supposed to be very familiar with the Old Testament. He was intelligent. Why do you think he had such a hard time understanding what Jesus was trying to tell him? Have you ever met someone who was very smart but seemed to be spiritually clueless? How do you think this happens?

Read 1 Corinthians 2:14. Did you find this verse to be true in your own life? What things about God did you have a hard time understanding before you gave your heart to Christ? Do they seem clearer now?

Read the quote by Anselm. Do you agree? Why, or why not?

> I do not seek to understand that I may believe, but I believe in order to understand. For this also I believe— that unless I believe, I should not understand.
>
> —Anselm

Why should Nicodemus have accepted Jesus' testimony about these spiritual matters?

How did Nicodemus eventually respond? (See John 7:50-51 and 19:39.)

Meditate on John 3:13-18

Read Numbers 21:4-9. This is the passage Jesus was referring to in John 3:14-15. How does this event illustrate Christ's redeeming work on the Cross and the need to believe in Him? Have there been times in your life when it was hard to believe? How did you overcome those times?

How do most people define *belief*? List several synonyms for *belief*. How does James 2:19 shape your definition? Why is belief necessary in order to gain eternal life? Why do you think true belief is so difficult?

> *It is so hard to believe because it is so hard to obey.*
>
> —*Søren Kierkegaard*

If we believe in Christ, what kind of life will we receive?

Does "eternal" refer only to the length of our lives, or do you think Jesus had something else in mind?

Read the quote by the 17th-century British clergyman Thomas Fuller. How are our lives changed when we truly believe in Christ? How has your life changed since you have become a Christian?

> *He does not believe that does not live according to his belief.* —*Thomas Fuller*

Why did God send Christ into the world? How does it make you feel to know that He loved you that much? What do you think it will take for people today to believe in Jesus? What are ways that you and your youth group can spread the gospel to the world?

PRAYER ☩ ASK AND LISTEN

Seek the face of God. Ask, "Lord, what are You saying to us today?"

Jesus calls us to be born again. He wants us to truly believe in the message that He sends us through His word. Ask Him for courage as you share your beliefs with others who don't know Him.

CONTEMPLATION  Reflect and Yield

Christ came to earth for the sole purpose of giving His life so anyone who believed in Him would be saved. Do you sometimes try to earn your salvation instead of trusting in what Christ has already done? Do you ever burden others with man-made requirements?

Group Study

- Have you been born again?

- What changes took place in your life when you were born again?

- Could your friends at school see evidence in your life that God has done something in you?

- What are ways you can increase your faith this week?

- How can your youth group help each other gain further knowledge on their own beliefs?

- Make a list of spiritual concepts you don't understand, or anything that keeps you from believing. As a group discuss those concepts and look to the Bible for answers to your questions.

SHARING THE GOOD NEWS
LISTENING FOR GOD THROUGH JOHN 4:4-24

SUMMARY

Whether it is in school, at soccer practice, or on the streets, we encounter people who are searching for happiness and meaning in life. If we looked beyond their outward appearance, we would find people struggling with addictions, dysfunctional families, and the consequences of poor choices. Some are trying desperately to fill the void in their lives, not realizing that these temporary fixes only add to their problems. What they need is Jesus.

In John 3, Jesus shares the way to eternal life with Nicodemus, a religious and moral man. But in John 4, Jesus offers life to someone who is the complete opposite of Nicodemus. The Samaritan woman is immoral, an outcast among outcasts. She doesn't come looking for Jesus; He comes looking for her.

Jesus provides us with a powerful example of how to overcome prejudice and share the Good News with those who need to hear it the most. He asks us to follow His example.

PREPARATION ☦ FOCUS YOUR THOUGHTS

Think about the television commercials you have seen this past week. Besides a particular product, what were they really trying to sell? What do these commercials reveal about what people are searching for in life?

READING ☦ HEAR THE WORD

In 722-721 B.C., the Northern Kingdom of Israel was destroyed by a fierce Assyrian army. The Assyrians took many Israelites into exile and repopulated the region with exiles from other conquered lands, forcing the groups of people to intermarry. Their descendants were known as Samaritans (from the name of the capital of the Northern Kingdom), half-breeds who were despised by the remaining Jews. Samaritans were considered inferior, unclean, and untouchable. Over the years, hatred between the Jews and Samaritans increased. The Samaritans tried to stop the rebuilding efforts of the Jews following the Babylonian captivity, and the Jews destroyed the Samaritan altar erected on Mount Gerizim in 128 B.C.

The Jews hated the Samaritans so much that they would take the longer route through Perea when traveling from one end of Israel to another. It was rare for a Jew to speak to a Samaritan, and touching an article handled by a Samaritan would make an item unclean. But Jesus broke all the religious norms of His day. He knew there was a Samaritan woman who needed what He had to offer, and He was compelled to travel to a town called Sychar to meet her.

Read John 4:4-24. If you are participating in a group, have members take turns reading one verse at a time. Read slowly and deliberately, trying to visualize the encounter as you read or listen.

MEDITATION ⚜ ENGAGE THE WORD

Meditate on John 4:4-9

What do these verses reveal about the compassion of Jesus? If you were tired, hungry, and thirsty, how would that affect your willingness to strike up a conversation with someone?

Why do you think Jesus asked the woman for a drink? How did it make the Samaritan woman feel?

Read the quote on page 34 by Benjamin Franklin. Have you ever asked a stranger for help? How did your request affect your relationship? Has a stranger ever asked you for help? How did you respond?

> *He that has done you a kindness will be more ready*
> *to do you another, than he whom you yourself have*
> *obliged.* —Benjamin Franklin

Jesus was in the region of Samaria, which was located between Galilee (to the north) and Judea (to the south), a place
devout Jews avoided. He was alone talking to a woman—and
a woman without morals, at that. What do you think the
religious leaders would have thought of Him if they had wit-
nessed Him talking to the woman?

What kinds of places or situations have you shied away from
for fear of what others might think? What types of people are
you tempted to avoid? Why? Would Jesus pass them by?

Meditate on John 4:10-15

How did Jesus fuel this woman's curiosity? What did He offer her? "Living water" was moving water fed by a spring, as
opposed to still water that had no movement. How is this a
fitting image for the Holy Spirit (see John 7:37-39)?

Why do you think the woman didn't understand? What was
she looking for?

Meditate on John 4:16-18

Why did Jesus tell the Samaritan woman to call her husband and come back when He already knew she didn't have one? What do you think went through her mind when Jesus said that? How do you think she felt when she realized Jesus knew all about her past? Why do you think she continued the conversation? Would you have reacted differently if you were in the position of the woman at the well?

Have you ever found yourself hoping Jesus wouldn't find out about something you've done?

Read the quote attributed to 15th-century French physicist and philosopher Blaise Pascal. How was this woman trying to fill the "God shaped vacuum" in her life? How do people to-day try to fill the emptiness in their lives? What is the result? (See the quote on page 36 by Marianne Williamson.)

> *There is a God shaped vacuum in the heart of each man which cannot be satisfied by any created thing, but only by God the creator made known through Jesus Christ.* —Blaise Pascal

> *Fill your mind with the meaningless stimuli of a world preoccupied with meaningless things, and it will not be easy to feel peace in your heart.*
>
> —Marianne Williamson

Meditate on John 4:19-24

Why did the woman bring up the disagreement between the Samaritans and Jews over where it was acceptable to worship? Think of a time when you tried to share with someone about Christ. What topics did the person bring up to distract you from the real issue—their need of a Savior? How did you deal with the diversion?

Jesus didn't compromise the truth; He acknowledged that salvation was from the Jews (because He himself came through the Jewish race, and the Jews had the testimony of the entire Old Testament; whereas the Samaritans used only the Pentateuch, the first five books of the Old Testament). But He also pointed to the bigger picture. Worship isn't about a place, but the attitude of the heart. The real question isn't *where do we worship?* but *how do we worship?*

What do you think it means to worship in "spirit and in truth" (4:24)?

PRAYER ⚜ ASK AND LISTEN

Seek the face of God. Ask, "Lord, what are You saying to us today?"

Ask the Lord to be with you as you share the gospel with others this week. Ask Him to break down the barriers of race and social class, and make you fully understand what it means to be part of the family of God. Trust that God will help you know what to say and how to say it.

CONTEMPLATION ⚜ REFLECT AND YIELD

Have you been harboring prejudice against groups of people because of race, age, economic background, gender, or religion? Are there people you don't want to witness to because you think they will reject the message? Are you willing to allow God to change your perspective?

GROUP STUDY

- Describe a time that you shared the gospel with someone.

- Is there someone in your life, possibly from a different background than yours, which God is asking you to talk to?

- Is there a "Samaria" in your life?

- Where does God want you to go in order to share His message?

- In what ways does our culture make it hard to over-look the differences in race, background and social standing, and realize that we are all God's children?

- Make a list of five things you could do this week to reach out to someone different from you.

THE TRUTH SHALL SET YOU FREE

LISTENING FOR GOD THROUGH JOHN 8:31-47

SUMMARY

Do you remember the movie, *The Matrix*? It was about the human race being enslaved to produce energy for a mechanical world. Their comfort was found through a simulated reality. What they saw as everyday life was, in fact, an illusion. They were tricked into believing they were free when they were actually slaves.

Many people today live in a similar matrix. They mistakenly think they are free—free to determine what is right and what is wrong, free to do as they please, free to decide what truth is and what it isn't, free to create their own destinies. They believe they are the gods of their own universe. Unfortunately, they are wrong. They have no understanding of the reality of life. They're enslaved, and they don't even know it.

Jesus came to reveal the truth. He came to set people free. In John 8:31-47, Jesus gave His listeners a black and white standard that isn't open to negotiation or individual interpretation—not even for us today.

PREPARATION ☦ FOCUS YOUR THOUGHTS

Can you remember a time when someone lied to you? How did it make you feel? Why do people lie? Are there times when people would rather hear a lie than hear the truth? When? Have you ever lied to someone to make them feel better? Is this type of lie different than any other type of lie?

READING ☦ HEAR THE WORD

John 7 shares of Jesus' teaching in the temple courts during the Feast of Tabernacles. Jews from around the world made the pilgrimage to Jerusalem for this great feast that celebrated Israel's deliverance from bondage in Egypt some 1,400 years earlier. Halfway through the feast, Jesus finally stepped up to teach. And He made quite an impression. The Jews were amazed at His teaching (7:15). Who could have taught Him these things? It is likely that the confrontation in 8:12-59 took place during this Feast of Tabernacles, even though John mentions the conclusion of the feast in 7:37.

While Jesus was teaching, "many put their faith in him" (8:30), He particularly addresses "the Jews who had believed him" (8:31). As Jesus shares the truth with them, it becomes clear that their belief is not a true and trusting faith. It hasn't fully penetrated their lives. Jesus helps them see that there is no middle ground when it comes to being a believer. Either you accept the truth, or you believe a lie. You are either a child of God and follow Him, or you are a child of the devil and reflect his character. There is nothing in between.

Read John 8:31-47. If involved in a group, take turns reading verses, but designate one person to read all the words of Jesus.

MEDITATION ✝ ENGAGE THE WORD

Meditate on John 8:31-36
According to these verses, what is the test for true discipleship? How does obedience to Jesus' teachings help us to know the truth? What is truth?

How do verses 8:36 and 14:6 affect your understanding of what Jesus is trying to say? Once we know the truth, in what ways are we set free?

Read the quote on page 42 by Madeleine L'Engle. What is the difference between truth and knowledge? Why do some people believe truth is whatever you want it to be? How do you see this concept influencing our culture? Do you see this creeping into the church? If so, how? Do you think Jesus meant for people to live like truth is whatever they want it to be?

> *Truth is eternal, knowledge is changeable. It is disastrous to confuse them.* —Madeleine L'Engle

Jewish teachers believed that because they had the Law, it was impossible for them to become slaves to sin. According to Romans 3:20, what was the purpose of the Old Testament law?

Why do you think the Jews reacted so strongly to Jesus' offer to be set free? They claimed never to have been slaves of anyone. Were they right? (Think of the feast they were celebrating.) Why do you think people fail to recognize or admit their enslavement? Have you been enslaved by something in your own life?

Have you ever heard people who profess to believe in God then make excuses for their lives of sin? List some of the sins that people are enslaved by today. Think about the sins that may be enslaving you?

What does the quote on page 43 by Ambrose Bierce say about the way the world views most religious people? How does it make you feel to know that people think of Christians in this light? What does Jesus mean when He says, "So, if the Son sets you free, you will be free indeed" (John 8:36)?

> Christian, n., One who follows the teachings of Christ insofar as they are not inconsistent with a life of sin.
>
> —Ambrose Bierce

What is your reaction to the quote by Hannah Whitall Smith?

> I believe it is inconsistent and disagreeable with true faith for people to be Christians, and yet to believe that Christ, the eternal Son of God, to whom all power in heaven and earth is given, will suffer sin and the devil to have dominion over them.
>
> —Hannah Whitall Smith

Meditate on John 8:37-42

The Jewish people were descendents of Abraham, but Jesus said that Abraham wasn't really their father. What do you think He meant by that? Is there a difference between being related by birth and being related spiritually? Do you have to be of the Jewish race to have Abraham as your father? (Read Rom. 2:28-29, Rom. 9:8, and Gal. 3:29.) What kind of a relationship do you have with your spiritual father?

Meditate on John 8:43-47

Jesus says if you aren't a child of Abraham, you're a child of the devil. How does Jesus describe the devil? Why does He describe him that way? How did the devil deceive Eve? How does the devil deceive people today? (See quote by William Shenstone.)

> *A liar begins with making falsehood appear like truth, and ends with making truth itself appear like falsehood.* —William Shenstone

Look at John 8:38 and 46. How do we know Jesus is sharing the truth, not simply one man's opinion? Why do people refuse to listen to Jesus today?

In John 8:43 Jesus accuses them of being unable to hear. What does it mean to hear God's Word? According to verse 47, why don't these people hear?

If we truly belong to God, how will people know? Why do you think Jesus uses such clear-cut terms?

PRAYER ✞ ASK AND LISTEN

Seek the face of God. Ask, "Lord, what are You saying to us today?"

Pray this prayer individually or together, "Search me, O God, and know my heart; test me and know my anxious thoughts. See if there is any offensive way in me, and lead me in the way everlasting" (Ps. 139:23-24). Wait a few minutes in silence for God to answer.

CONTEMPLATION ☩ REFLECT AND YIELD

Can other people tell by your actions whose child you are?

Christ came to set us free from sin. Is there some sin you need to surrender to Him today?

Are you struggling to accept the truth of His Word? Settle it right now, and determine to listen and obey.

GROUP STUDY

- What was your life like before you knew Christ, and you were a slave to sin?

- If a mirror was held up to your life, what kind of reflection would you see?

- How does our culture contribute to the idea of, "truth is whatever I want it to mean"?

- Has your youth group become burdened by the enslavement of sin? What can you do as a group to release those chains?

- What are the ways we can seek God's truth and avoid false teachings?

- As a group, make a commitment to spend at least 15 minutes each day this week reading the Bible. Keep a list of everything God reveals to you, and start obeying.

THE SHEPHERD AND HIS SHEEP

LISTENING FOR GOD THROUGH JOHN
10:1-16, 27-29

SUMMARY

A healthy looking youth strums on a harp while relaxing under the shade of an oak tree. His sheep graze peacefully nearby. The setting is calm. Although this is the picture most of us form when envisioning a shepherd, it's not an accurate reflection of shepherding in Jesus' day. The hillsides surrounding Jerusalem were rocky, and vegetation was sparse. Water was limited. Shepherds often faced danger from wild animals and thieves who saw sheep as easy prey. Good shepherds took their jobs seriously and risked their own lives for the protection of their flock.

In the Old Testament, God described himself as a Shepherd for His people (Ps. 23:1, Isa. 40:10-11, and Ezek. 34:11-16). And the kings of Israel, as His representatives, were also supposed to act as shepherds. But instead of protecting the flock, they abandoned the Lord, led the people into sin, and subjected them to disaster.

So God promised to send a Good Shepherd for His people—the Messiah. The true sheep would recognize Him immediately.

PREPARATION ☦ FOCUS YOUR THOUGHTS

How does it make you feel when someone you haven't seen in a long time remembers your name, or when someone you barely know calls you by name?

Who in your life has a unique voice that you always recognize?

READING ☦ HEAR THE WORD

Jesus' illustration of the shepherd and the sheep exposed the truth behind the Pharisees and religious leaders. Even though they were supposed to be watching out for the welfare of God's people, they showed no compassion or responsibility. This was especially apparent after their treatment of the man born blind (but healed by Jesus) in chapter 9 and their prior determination to kick out of the synagogue anyone who acknowledged that Jesus was the Messiah (John 9:22).

The imagery of the shepherd was familiar. During the cold

winter months, sheep were often kept inside at night. Several flocks occupied one pen, and a watchman was assigned to guard the gate until the shepherds returned. Only the shepherd had rightful access to the sheep. Though sheep were not the brightest animals, they readily recognized their own shepherd's voice and followed when he called.

In John 10:11-18 Jesus shows the difference between the genuine, sacrificial love of the shepherd, and the self-interest of the hired hand.

Jesus also compares himself to the single gate that provided access to the sheep, illustrating the necessity of going through Him in order to be saved. Here the focus turns to the sheep, which must be *His* sheep and must enter *His* way. Jesus clearly defines those who are His.

Read John 10:1-16, 27-29 silently. If you are participating in a group, have someone read the passages out loud while everyone else closes their eyes. Try to visualize the scenes.

MEDITATION ✝ ENGAGE THE WORD

Meditate on John 10:2-6

What are some characteristics of the shepherd mentioned in these verses? How is the role of the shepherd different from the cowboy you've seen in western movies or television shows?

Why would a shepherd bother to name all his sheep? How does it make you feel to realize Jesus knows your name? Can you think of other verses that reveal how God is intimately connected with us?

What two traits define the sheep? What does it mean for us to know the Shepherd's voice? How do we learn to recognize it?

Do you agree with the quote by Hannah Whitall Smith? What are some other ways we hear God's voice today? In what ways does the Shepherd (Jesus) expect us to follow Him? What are the advantages of following the Shepherd? What are the consequences of not following? Read Psalm 23. Why would any sheep *not* follow the Good Shepherd?

> There are four special ways in which God speaks: by the voice of Scripture, the voice of the inward impressions of the Holy Spirit, the voice of our own higher judgment, and the voice of providential circumstances.
>
> —Hannah Whitall Smith

Jesus told us to run away when we hear a stranger's voice. Who or what does the stranger represent? What does it mean to run away? Describe an experience when you met a stranger who tried to lead you away from the Shepherd. Is it a possibility that some of your peers at school represent the stranger? How did you respond?

Meditate on John 10:1, 7-10

Who were the thieves and robbers Jesus was referring to? In what way were they refusing to enter by the gate? How did they steal and kill and destroy the flock?

In contrast, how does Jesus treat His sheep (10:9)? What does He offer (10:10)? What does it mean to have life "to the full" (10:10)?

Do you know anyone who is trying to be saved through a way other than by coming through the Gate (Christ)? To whom or to what are they looking for salvation? How can you explain to them the benefits of following the Shepherd and warn them of the dangers of following robbers?

Meditate on John 10:11-16

Here Jesus contrasts the Good Shepherd with the hired hand. What's the difference? Have you seen this principle in life today, perhaps when an employer and his employees demonstrate different priorities regarding work? What are the main concerns of each? As the Good Shepherd, what is Jesus willing to do for His sheep? Why would He do that? How does that make you feel?

Discuss the quote by Hannah Whitall Smith. Can you think of any examples of something a Christian might gladly do for money but not for Christ? Why do you think money is such a powerful motivator for some people? What should be our motivation for following Christ and caring for one another? Which should be more persuasive?

> And I am ashamed to think that any Christian should ever put on a long face and shed tears over doing a thing for Christ, which a worldly man would be only too glad to do for money.
>
> —Hannah Whitall Smith

Meditate on John 10:27-29

Verses 3-4, 14, 16, and 27, define *sheep*. How do we know if someone is truly one of Jesus' sheep? What assurance does Jesus give concerning His sheep in verse 28? The Greek word for *snatch* in verses 28 and 29 is also found in 10:12, where it is translated *attack*. What did Jesus mean when He says no one can snatch them out of His hand (10:28)?

Read the quote on page 53 by Frederick Louis Godet. How does it change the way you understand these verses? Is it possible for a sheep to walk away from the Shepherd?

The question is of enemies from without who seek to carry off the sheep, but not of unfaithfulness through which the sheep would themselves cease to be sheep.

—Frederick Louis Godet

PRAYER ♰ ASK AND LISTEN

Seek the face of God. Ask, "Lord, what are You saying to us today?"

Jesus wants to be your Shepherd. If you are His sheep, you must listen to His voice and follow where He leads. Ask God to help you recognize His voice today.

CONTEMPLATION ♰ REFLECT AND YIELD

Have you been guilty of listening to other voices, rather than to the voice of Jesus? Are you willing to start listening and following?

GROUP STUDY

- What are ways you need the Good Shepherd to move in your life?

- How can we make sure that we follow the Shepherd and not the stranger?

- What are some examples of the voices that we hear every day?

- How can we distinguish the voice of Jesus from all other voices?

- What are the ways Jesus speaks to us?

- Do you listen to the voice of Jesus when He calls you? When you hear it, what is your reaction?

- As a group, make a commitment to spend 5 to 10 minutes each morning this week listening for God's voice. Don't say anything, just listen. As you gather together after the week has passed, share what God has been saying to you.

ASSURANCE OF HEAVEN AND THE HOLY SPIRIT
LISTENING FOR GOD THROUGH JOHN 14:1-6, 15-21, 25-27

SUMMARY

Every time we turn on the television or read the newspapers we hear about the latest tragedies—wars, bombings, murders, accidents, kidnappings, abuses, and diseases. The casual observer is tempted to believe that an uncaring God has abandoned the world or that He is unable to control the decline of civilization. Our hearts can easily become troubled by the uncertainty of the future and the possibility of pain for ourselves and our families. But troubling times are nothing new. In fact, Jesus confirmed, "In this world you *will* have trouble" (John 16:33, emphasis added). Trouble is a certainty—but being troubled isn't. We can have peace in the middle of our hardest times.

The struggles of life increase our longing for heaven. And heaven is a certainty. Jesus said it was. The Holy Spirit is the guarantee that heaven is waiting for us. We haven't been left alone as orphans. Our God is with us through every trial—through every tragedy—in the person of the Holy Spirit living within us. And if you don't have that assurance, you can.

PREPARATION ☦ FOCUS YOUR THOUGHTS

What do you think heaven will be like? What do you imagine you will do there?

Make a list of four or five things that you can't see, but you still believe are real.

READING ☦ HEAR THE WORD

Just days earlier, Jesus had been welcomed into Jerusalem by crowds of worshipers gathered for the upcoming Passover celebration. They had waved palm branches and shouted, "Hosanna!" Excitement had filled the air as word spread that Jesus raised Lazarus from the dead in nearby Bethany. But Jesus knew the admiration wouldn't last. He knew His crucifixion was at hand.

John 13-17 is the most extensive record in the Gospels of the events taking place the night before Jesus' crucifixion. Jesus washed the disciples' feet showing love and servitude. Later

He told them that He would die, He would be betrayed by one of the Twelve, and that Peter would disown Him three times before morning. The disciples were understandably troubled. This wasn't what they were expecting. And so Jesus speaks words of comfort and assurance to His disappointed followers.

Slowly read John 14:1-6, 15-21, and 25-27. If you're reading as a group, take turns reading.

MEDITATION ✠ ENGAGE THE WORD

Meditate on John 14:1-6

What does Jesus mean when He speaks of His Father's house? The word for *rooms* literally means *dwelling places* (translated *home* in 14:23). Why is it important that He mentioned the Father's house having many rooms?

Read Ephesians 2:21-22. In John 14:1-6, do you think Jesus is speaking about heaven or of His coming into our lives in a personal relationship? Or is it possible that He has both in view? (See Heb. 8:5; 9:11; and Rev. 11:19; 15:5.)

In John 14:3, Jesus promises to go to prepare a place and then to come back for them. Which of the following do you think He is referring to: going to the Cross and coming back after the Resurrection; going into heaven at the Ascension and then coming back at the Second Coming; or something else?

How does focusing on heaven (or on our relationship with Christ) help our hearts to be untroubled? (Read the quote by Bob Snyder.)

> *Our destination is home with our Father in heaven. It is so easy on this journey to lose sight of our destination and to focus on the detours of this life instead. This life is only the trip to get home.* —*Bob Snyder*

Read John 14:6. During hard times, how does knowing that Jesus is the one and only way, and not one way among many, give you certainty?

Meditate on John 14:15-21

How does Jesus describe the Holy Spirit? Can you think of any situations in the Old Testament where the Holy Spirit empowered an individual? How is the role of the Holy Spirit described in the Old Testament different from what Jesus describes here?

In Acts 2 God sent the Holy Spirit to fill and empower all the believers at Pentecost. Does He still do that today? How? When? (See Rom. 8:9.)

How does Jesus compare himself with the Holy Spirit in these verses? How is His presence a comfort and help in times of trial? How have you received comfort and help during specific circumstances in your own life?

How do we show Jesus that we really love Him (14:15, 21)? What do you think Jesus means when He says of one who loves Him, "I, too, will love him and show myself to him" (14:21)? How does Jesus reveal himself to us on a daily basis?

Read 1 Corinthians 2:9-10. How does the Holy Spirit make heavenly realities known to us?

Read 2 Corinthians 1:22; 5:5; and Ephesians 1:4. What does the Holy Spirit *guarantee* for us? How do we know for sure that the Holy Spirit dwells within us (Rom. 8:16)?

Read the quote by Gordon MacDonald. How will the Holy Spirit make his presence known if He is truly in us?

> One quickly gains a sense from the Bible that wherever the Holy Spirit is found in the lives of people, strange and wonderful things are likely to happen at any moment.   —Gordon MacDonald

Meditate on John 14:25-27

What is the role of the Holy Spirit? In what ways did the Holy Spirit teach and remind the disciples? In what ways does He still do that today for us? Does this cancel out our responsibility to read and study the Word or to listen to pastors and teachers? Why, or why not?

How would you define "peace"? How is the peace Jesus offers different from what the world offers? How does our culture portray peace? Is it even possible to find peace through the world? According to Philippians 4:6-7, how do we gain peace?

Do you agree with the quote by A. W. Tozer? Can you put it in your own words? Why would separating our lives into specific sections deprive us of peace? On a scale of 1 to 10 (10 being the highest), how much peace do you have on a daily basis? Do you notice yourself dividing your life into sacred and secular?

> One of the great hindrances to internal peace that the Christian encounters is the common habit of dividing our lives into two areas—the sacred and the secular.
>
> —A. W. Tozer

PRAYER ☦ ASK AND LISTEN

Seek the face of God. Ask, "Lord, what are You saying to us today?"

Ask God to help you release the burdens you carry. Cast your anxieties on Him right now. If you are praying with a partner, ask how you can specifically pray for their needs. Together, lift your burdens to God and ask Him to give you peace.

CONTEMPLATION ⚜ REFLECT AND YIELD

In what ways do people become materialistic or worldly in their perspectives of heaven? Are you ever tempted to think of heaven as a place where you can have everything you want? What makes it heaven? How can you experience a taste of true heaven right where you are today?

GROUP STUDY

- How has Jesus revealed himself to you lately?

- Do you have a hard time understanding who the "Holy Spirit" is?

- What questions do you have about the Holy Spirit and His presence in your life?

- How do you receive peace? Is it easy for you to give your anxieties to God when you are going through a stressful time? Why or why not?

- How do you overcome viewing heaven through a worldly perspective?

- Make a list of all the things that trouble your spirit. Pray over those things as a group and individually, and ask the Holy Spirit to give you peace.

REMAINING IN THE VINE
LISTENING FOR GOD THROUGH JOHN 15:1-7

SUMMARY

Jesus came to reveal the Father and to show us the way to a personal relationship with Him. Seven times in John's Gospel Jesus says, "I am . . . ," and follows with an illustration that reveals both who He is and how we should respond. ("I Am" was the covenant name for God, revealed in Exodus 3:14. But Jesus applies it to himself in John 8:58.) Jesus is the Bread of Life (6:48) we depend on for our sustenance; the Light of the World (8:12) we reflect; the Gate (10:9) we must enter through; the Good Shepherd (10:11) we follow; the Resurrection and the Life (11:25) we place our hope in; the Way, the Truth, and the Life (14:6) we believe and obey. And now, in 15:1, He describes himself as the Vine.

Jesus reveals to us the only way to faithfully live out the
Christian life. We must remain in Him. We must maintain a
consistent, unshakable relationship with Christ. It's not begin-
ning well that counts most; it's living and ending well.

PREPARATION ♱ FOCUS YOUR THOUGHTS

In ten years, do you think you will have the same friends that
you do now? Why or why not? Are your friends from school
and youth group the type that will last a lifetime? Why, or
why not? What determines whether you keep in touch with
someone?

How do your friendships affect your behavior or attitude?

READING ♱ HEAR THE WORD

The symbol of the vine was familiar to Jews living in Jesus'
day. Vineyards were common, and the knowledge of how
to care for them and prune them was widespread. As Jesus
and His disciples set out from the Upper Room and made
their way to the Mount of Olives, there is no doubt that they
passed several. Maybe it was passing the ornate golden vine
that decorated the entrance to the Temple that provoked Jesus' illustration.

In the Old Testament the nation of Israel was often compared
to a vine—although at some points it might be a useless,

unproductive one. So, when Jesus announces He is the "true vine," He is certainly claiming to be the true Israel. But unlike faithless Israel, He is not lacking in any way. He is the source of life for all who remain in Him.

In chapter 15 Jesus uses the word *remain* (*abide* in the KJV) 11 times. In John's Gospel it is used a total of 40 times. Even in John's Epistles it occurs 27 times. Do you get the impression the word is important? Remaining in the vine is the secret to a vibrant, productive, fruitful Christian life. It is also the secret to answered prayer.

Jesus never meant for us to have a casual relationship with Him. He meant for us to be constantly abiding in Him.

Slowly read aloud John 15:1-17. If you are in a group, join together in reading the word *remain* whenever it occurs.

MEDITATION ✟ ENGAGE THE WORD

Meditate on John 15:1-8

Who is the gardener? What is His purpose in pruning the vine? When have you felt the pruning hand of God in your life? Was it painful or pleasant? What was the result?

The Greek word for *prune* also means *clean*. How does that, along with Jesus' words in 13:10, affect your understanding of 15:3?

What does it mean to remain in Christ? How do we do it? What are the indicators that someone is not remaining in Christ? What is the consequence? How does Luke 13:6-9 affect your understanding of this passage?

In John 15:2 and 5, Jesus talks about bearing fruit. What is the fruit of a Christian? Read Galatians 5:22-23 and the quote by Agnew.

> The fruit of the Spirit is the harvest, marking growth and maturity. It produces ethical character. It is the true measure of holiness of life and practice in the believer. Every believer is expected to bear fruit.
>
> —Milton S. Agnew

On a scale of 1 to 10 (1 being the lowest), how fruitful do you consider yourself? How satisfied are you with your level of fruitfulness? What can you do to become more fruitful?

Do you agree with the quote by Robert Foster? What does he mean by focusing on the foliage instead of the root system?

> *The man who concentrates on the root system of his life is going to bear fruit upward, but if he concentrates on the eye-appealing foliage he may end up a rootless failure.* —Robert D. Foster

Read verses 7 and 8. If we are remaining in Christ, for what kinds of things will we pray? What do you usually pray for? In what ways does God receive glory through our fruitfulness?

Meditate on John 15:9-17

How are love and obedience connected?

What are some substantial ways we can show love for other Christians? How did Jesus demonstrate His love for people? Do you think He really expects us to give up our lives for one another? Why, or why not? Is there anyone you would die for? Consider this question silently: Who would I not be willing to die for?

What is the result of obedience to Christ's commands? What is the difference between joy and happiness?

If you don't feel joy in your heart, how can you obtain it today?

> The miracle of the joy of God has nothing to do with a man's life or his circumstances or the condition he is in. Jesus does not come to a man and say "Cheer up." He plants within a man the miracle of the joy of God's own nature.   —Oswald Chambers

What do you consider the five most important qualities in a friend? What does Jesus say is different between being a friend and being a servant?

What "business" of His has Jesus revealed to us? (See John 15:15.) Which two Old Testament figures were considered friends of God (see Exod. 33:11 and Isa. 41:8)? Why do you think they were described that way? What does it mean to be a friend of Jesus?

What do you think it means to pray in Jesus' name (John 15:16)? Notice the word *then* in the middle of verse 16. What condition does Jesus give for answered prayer? What should Christians be praying for? What could you do to make your prayers more powerful and effective? (See James 5:15-16.)

PRAYER ✠ ASK AND LISTEN

Seek the face of God. Ask, "Lord, what are You saying to us today?"

God appointed us to bear fruit. He expects it of us. Ask God today to prune you to make you more fruitful. Then pray for a person in your youth group or church congregation.

CONTEMPLATION ✠ REFLECT AND YIELD

Are you actively cultivating your relationship with Christ? How can you draw closer to Him? Are you afraid of the pruning process or what He might ask of you? Trust Him. He has your best interests at heart. Let go of anything hindering your walk with Christ.

GROUP STUDY

- What does the symbol of Jesus as the vine mean to you?

- Is it hard for you to remain in the vine? Why, or why not?

- What type of fruit do you bear as a Christian?

- In what ways would non-believers know that you are bearing this fruit?

- Reflect on the seven "I Am" statements: "I am the Bread of Life", "I am the Light of the World," etc. Which description impacts you the most?

- List four or five specific actions you can take this week to remain in Christ. Discuss these as a group.

JESUS PRAYS FOR US
LISTENING FOR GOD THROUGH JOHN 17:1-5, 14-19, 20-23

SUMMARY

It's no secret that there is great division in the Body of Christ. Different denominations are everywhere, disagreeing over doctrines and practical expressions of the Christian faith. Even within individual churches, members are often at odds with one another. All the arguing over inconsequential matters distracts us from the mission of the Church in the world.

This is not what Jesus had in mind. He prayed that all believers would be one, just as He and the Father are one. But the oneness wouldn't be achieved by preaching a watered-down message, or by lowering standards to make everyone comfortable. The oneness would be achieved as every Christian became one with Christ, sanctified by the truth of God's Word. We see so little unity in the Church today because we see so little of Christ.

If we can accomplish what Jesus prayed for, the world will stand up and take notice; people will realize Jesus really was divine and that He really can change lives.

May it begin in us today.

PREPARATION ☦ FOCUS YOUR THOUGHTS

What team sports do you now play or have you played in the past? What was/is your favorite game's objective? How does a team work together to accomplish it? What is the secret to being good at that sport?

READING ☦ HEAR THE WORD

John 17 is popularly known as Jesus' "High Priestly Prayer," a prayer of intercession for himself, His disciples, and all believers. Jesus mentioned several times during His ministry that His time had not yet come (John 2:4; 7:6, 8, 30; 8:20). But now "the time has come" (17:1). It's time for Him to go to the Cross, to suffer and die for the sins of the whole world. His arrest and crucifixion are about to happen. His followers need this prayer to help them through what lies ahead.

Many instances are recorded in the Gospels where Jesus prayed. In what we know as "The Lord's Prayer," He gave His disciples a pattern so they could learn to pray. But this prayer in John 17 is also an example for us. It is Jesus' longest recorded prayer. And what He prays in the hours before His arrest tells us a lot concerning what was on His heart. These same passions should be on our hearts.

Place yourself in a position of prayer (head bowed, kneeling, etc.) as you read Jesus' prayer. Read slowly and thoughtfully. If you are in a group have one person read 17:1-5, have another read verses 14-19, and have another read verses 20-23.

MEDITATION ✠ ENGAGE THE WORD

Meditate on John 17:1-5

How many times does Jesus use the word *glory*, or *glorify*, in this passage? What does it mean to "glorify" someone? How did Jesus glorify God? What was the "work" God had given Him to do? Why do you think Jesus said He had already completed God's work when He hadn't yet gone to the Cross?

How can you bring glory to God through your life? What work has God called you to do?

How does Jesus define *eternal life* in verse 3? How is this definition different from what you previously thought? What difference does it make if you stress eternal *life* as opposed to *eternal* life?

Meditate on John 17:14-19

In praying for His disciples, Jesus says that the world hated them. What evidence is there for His statement? Why did the world hate them? What does it mean to be "of the world" (17:14)? How can we be "in the world" and relate to the world without being "of the world"?

In what ways is the Church doing well in this area? In what ways is it doing poorly?

What does it mean to be "sanctified"? The Greek word used here also can be translated "set apart for sacred use" or "made holy." What does that add to your understanding of the term?

How does the truth of God's Word sanctify us? (See Rom. 12:1-2.) Why would Jesus need to sanctify himself?

Read the quote by Andrew Murray. How does it help you to understand your responsibility in sanctification?

> *Many of God's children long for a better life, but do not realize the need of giving God time day by day in their inner chamber by the Spirit to renew and sanctify their lives.* —Andrew Murray

When we are sanctified, or set apart, in what ways are we noticeably different from the world around us? Why does that cause the world to hate us?

What people hate you right now because of your stand for the truth of God's Word? Have you ever had someone at school give you a hard time because of what you believe? How did you handle that situation? How does it make you feel to know that Jesus already prayed for your protection (John 17:15)?

Read the quote by Tertullian. If all Christians have the same Bible, why do they sometimes disagree over what "truth" is? Why is it important to know the truth?

> *Christ laid down one definite system of truth which the world must believe without qualification, and which we must seek precisely in order to believe it when we find it.*
>
> *—Tertullian*

Meditate on John 17:20-23

Jesus wants us to be united, and He makes it possible for us to be united. Why, then, do Christians have such a hard time getting along? What does it mean to be "in unity"? Why is it so important that Christians are united?

Read the quote by Bob Snyder. What is the secret to unity in the Body of Christ? What difference would it make in your family, in your church, in your neighborhood, and in our world if Christians were united for the cause of Christ?

> *Christian unity is not found in uniformity, organization, or a particular church, but rather in Jesus and our commitment to His teachings, and living them out in our lives. . . . It is only as we join together with others who look different than we do but share a common love and commitment to the Truth that is Jesus, that we can know the completeness of the body of Christ.*
>
> *—Bob Snyder*

PRAYER ☩ ASK AND LISTEN

Seek the face of God. Ask, "Lord, what are You saying to us today?"

Ask Jesus to help you bring glory to God by living a sanctified life committed to truth. Search His Word so you are living in the world, but not of the world.

CONTEMPLATION ☩ REFLECT AND YIELD

How can you promote Christian unity? Is there a strained relationship God wants you to mend?

Are you sanctified (set apart for God's use) completely? What is He calling you to do or to become? Are you willing to follow, even if it means others may hate you?

GROUP STUDY

- Is it a challenge for you to be in the world and not of the world?

- What comes to mind when you hear the word "sanctification"?

- How are you set apart from the world? Is it noticeable to non-believers?

- Since Jesus wants us to be united, why is it sometimes hard for the people in your church, or even in your own youth group to get along?

- Are you united as a youth group? What are you lacking?

- How have the Words of Jesus written in the Book of John made a difference in your life? How will it affect your faith journey from this point forward?

CPSIA information can be obtained
at www.ICGtesting.com
Printed in the USA
LVHW082212070123
736699LV00004B/297

9 780834 150225